Discovering Red

a children's book about the color red

by Tracy Lee

Want bilingual children's products?
Keep up with us!

🌐 heymeimei.com

📷 @heymeimei

ISBN: 978-1-960025-05-0

For my little Kai Kai.

apple

balloon

cherries

firecracker

firetruck

heart

ladybug

mushroom

pepper

red crayon

rose

strawberry

tomato

watermelon

mask

red envelope

steak

lobster

This book is all about red,

From cherries to tomatoes, it's said.

Ladybugs, balloons and more,

We'll explore the color red, for sure!

apple

Red apples, crisp and round,
a healthy snack, to be found.

firetruck

Red fire trucks, bright and bold,
ready to save, young and old.

balloon

Red balloons, tied with string,
a playful sight, flying high.

cherries

Red cherries, plucked with glee,
a tasty treat for you and me.

heart

Red hearts, big and small, a symbol of love, for one and all.

ladybug

Red ladybugs, with black spots,
a colorful bug, that flies a lot.

pepper

Red peppers, spicy and bold, handle with care, or your mouth will scold.

mask

A red mask, worn with pride, a symbol of courage, on the inside.

mushroom

Red mushrooms, small and round,
hiding in the forest, to be found.

red crayon

With a red crayon, we color with glee,
it's as red as an apple, as red as can be!

watermelon

Red watermelons, big and bright,
a juicy snack, what a delight!

lobster

The red lobster with its shell so bright, in the ocean it's a beautiful sight.

rose

Red roses are pretty, happy and bright, some say it's love at first sight.

tomato

Red tomatoes, on a vine, a summer treat, that's just divine.

red envelope

Red envelopes, filled with cash, a gift and a fortune, of epic proportions.

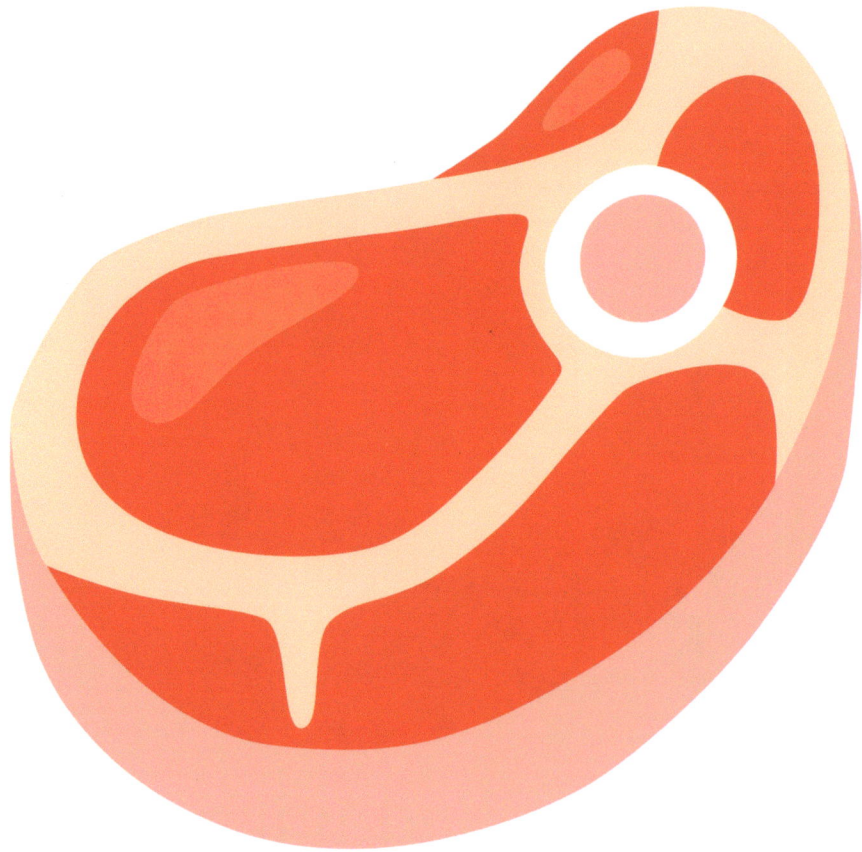

steak

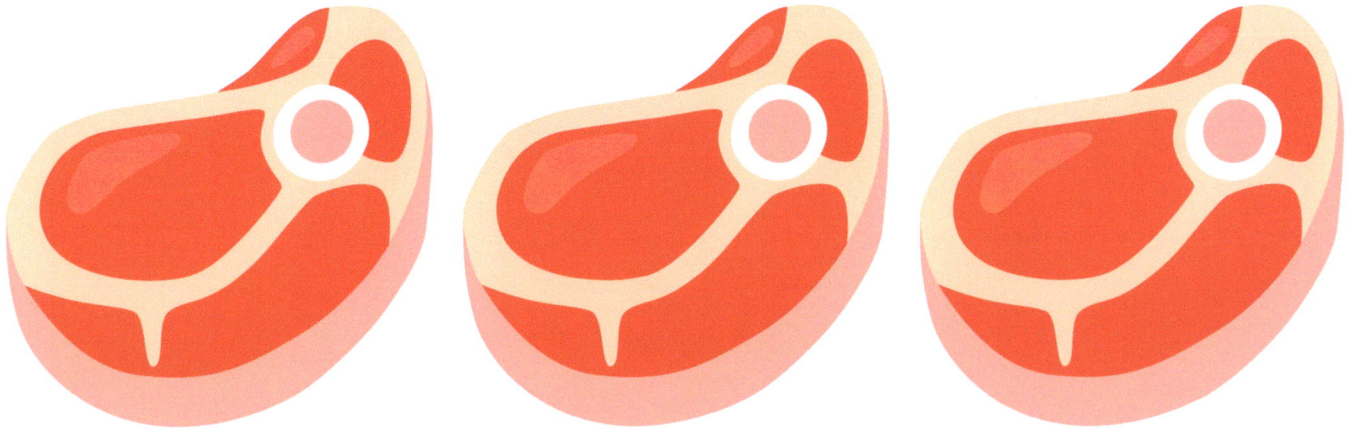

A juicy red steak, on the plate it does sit, a tasty treat that's hard to resist!

strawberry

Red strawberries, plump and sweet, a delicious treat to eat.

firecracker

Red firecrackers, loud and bright, a
fun surprise, on a celebratory night.

 apple

 balloon

 cherries

 firecracker

 firetruck

 heart

 ladybug

 mushroom

 pepper

 red crayon

 rose

 strawberry

 tomato

 watermelon

 mask

 red envelope

 steak

 lobster

Red is a color we now know well,

Like red envelopes and roses, so swell,

Watermelon and strawberries too,

Exploring red ahead is what we'll do!

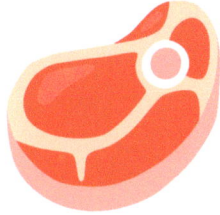

www.ingramcontent.com/pod-product-compliance
Lightning Source LLC
LaVergne TN
LVHW072053070426

835508LV00002B/79

9 781960 025050